satín the

traveling mutt

Author :

ROXANA CONRADO

Illustrated by:

ROLANDO MARTÍNEZ
DANIEL REYES

Visit us in Facebook / Instagram: *@satinelviajero*
Email: *satinelviajerosato@gmail.com*

ISBN: 978-0-9992867-2-2
Made in United States of America

Author's Note

"Satín, the Traveling Mutt" offers us a world where values like honesty, love, and the beautiful things in life are presented, through each character, to teach their importance to our children. Knowledge and interior beauty play a leading role, and encourage them to explore a new world. We hope that, through the travels of Satín, they will learn important human values to help them grow and navigate life. Lessons and emotions fill the traveler's journeys and he, Satín, will be their traveling companion forever.

Once upon a time, in a little kingdom deep inside the forest, there was a little mutt, a stray dog, who was always leaping and running happily through the alleyways of the kingdom. Satín, the very mutty mutt, told everyone he met that he would conquer the world!

Most people laughed at him, while others just looked away. But Satín, the little mutt, dreamed of the conquests and treasures that awaited him.

One very, very rainy day, Satín decided to visit his friend, a turtle named Beauty. Even though she was very slow, she was very, very wise. The very mutty mutt had a great big question in his head and he thought that his friend, who knew everything, could help him find the answer.

– Tell me, Beauty the Turtle, how many days will it take me to conquer the world?

– The world? Do you have any idea how big the world is?

A thunderous belly-laugh was heard through the window. Satín's ears perked up, he stood up on all fours, sniffed the air, and looked around to see who was laughing at him.

– Hahaaaaaaa, HAHAHAHAAAAAA, HAHAHahaaaaa…
You, Satín the Conqueror! Hahahaaaaa

It was none other than Brutos, the chief dog of the Royal Guard. Famous for his bravery and skill in battle, admirer of beautiful lady dogs, and suitor of young lasses.

Satín, hearing his mocking laughter, said to him:

Well, do you know how big the world is?

– The world? The world is this kingdom! The world is the beautiful lady dogs who cross my path. – Responded Brutos, watching a pretty little dog as she crossed his path.

– Ha! The beautiful lady dogs may be your world, but the world is more than that, and I will show you. Isn't that right, Beauty the Turtle?
       – Insisted Satín.

– The world goes far beyond the borders of the kingdom. In the world there are many kingdoms where there are different foods, dances, music, where other languages are spoken, and where many kinds of plants and animals live. – Beauty the Turtle explained.

– Yeah, right, Beauty the Turtle... you and your stories that nobody can possibly prove. – Replied Brutos angrily.

– Well, I'm going to prove them! – Satín declared with determination.

– Oh, yeah? We'll see how far you get with your weak little body. Hahahaha! – Brutos laughed at the traveler.

Brutos boasted of his svelte physique and spent his time working out. He stopped at every stream he came upon and, once he was finished drinking from it and admiring his own reflection in the water, he would ask it:

– Tell me, honest stream, who is the most beautiful of them all?

– Brutos, Brutos…I told you before…you will find out soon!
  – The honest stream would reply.

And every time Brutos heard this reply, he would fill with rage and work out even more. He would run up and down the mountains, swim across the river, and walk through the woods without resting. When he arrived at the palace, he would run up and down the stairs ten times every day. He was certainly a strong dog, focused on building his muscles so he would be admired by all the beauties in the kingdom.

Goaded by the mocking challenge that Brutos had given him, Satín decided to set out on his adventure to see the world. He asked Beauty the Turtle for a map, a compass, and a notebook so he could write down the stories from his journey. He went home and took a photo with his parents and his siblings so he could have something to remember them by.

He found a pair of dark sunglasses to protect him from the sun, and a scarf in case it got cold. With everything ready, he asked his mother to wish him luck as he set out on his travels. He said goodbye to Beauty the Turtle and told her that he would be living proof of all the stories she had told.

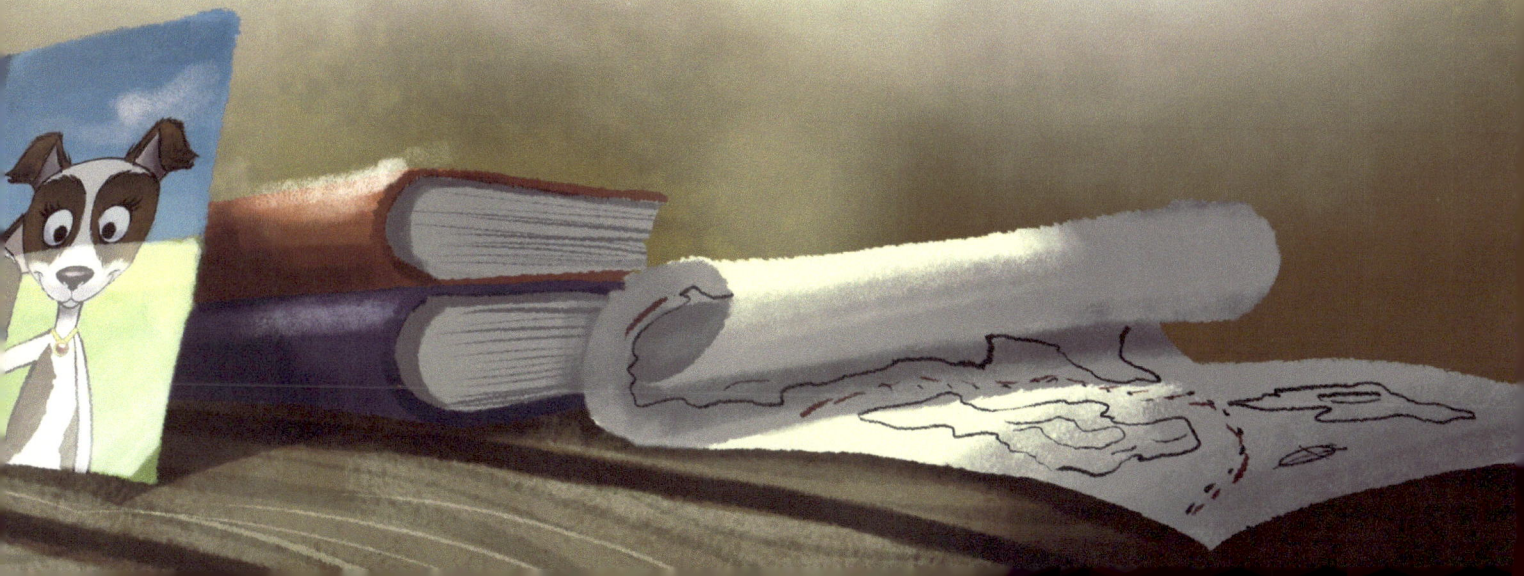

The cry resounded throughout the kingdom, shouts of joy and songs full of emotion sent the traveler on his way:

Satín, the traveling mutt!
Satín, the eternal traveler.
Satín, come back to your kingdom... and tell us the story!
Tra-la-la-la...tra-la-la-la-la

And so our Satín, the very mutty mutt, set off to experience and conquer the world.

It was the first day of his journey, and it was splendid. Everything was brilliant and beautiful. The mutty mutt was happy because he was on his way to complete a very important mission for the kingdom. He wrote in his notebook about all his favorite moments, and at the end of each day, he made his report.

On the map, he marked the names of the places he visited. Satín followed the colored lines that Beauty the Turtle had drawn to show him the safest roads. Roads that would take him to famous places where he would encounter a totally new world.

Along the way he discovered smells and tastes that nobody in his kingdom had ever smelled or tasted. Like a good explorer, he studied where they came from. He smelled the ocean for the first time, and saw how incredibly huge it was. He plunged into it, and jumped and played and became covered in sand too. High above him, on top of a rock, they watched him. An iguana laughed at the sight of him and said:

– Hey, traveler, haven't you ever seen the ocean before?

– Well, no. We don't have an ocean where I come from. – Replied the traveler. And you? Who are you?

– My name is Blue! – The iguana said from far away.

– Blue? But you're green! – The very mutty mutt replied, looking at him with surprise.

– Yes, I know, but my mother is color-blind, so I don't look green to her. So where are you going?

– I'm going to see the whole world. I'm on a mission for my kingdom!
        – Satín replied excitedly.

– A mission, you say? – Blue asked him, full of curiosity.

– Yes, I'm going in search of places where I can find new foods, other languages, and new music!

Blue, bursting with joy, said to him:

– Party! What you want is a party! Yaaaayyyyy!... My friend, you've come to the best kingdom. I'm going to introduce you to a couple of heron friends who will teach you to dance, and with the otter, you'll play guitar.

– **Really?** – Asked the very mutty mutt.

– **I'm as serious as the sky is blue!**
    – Replied the iguana, and they headed off together.

Blue walked with Satín, the mutty mutt, and he told him all about that kingdom. They walked together for several days and nights, visiting the important places and learning the history of them all. Their time was filled with music, dance, theaters, and museums. One final goodbye surprise awaited him on his last night in the kingdom.

With his new friend Satín, Blue entered the party hall.

– Hello, dear. Blue says that you are a traveler?
     – Said the older heron upon seeing him.

– Yes, I am on a mission for my kingdom. – Replied the traveler.

– Mission, mission, mission… NO! I don't want to hear about missions tonight. We're going to dance, party, and sing. We're going to teach this traveler how we dance in this kingdom…right…left…and a little step forward…and a little step backward…and move your hips to the beat of the music… – The older heron said, raising his voice.

– The otter entered the hall with his guitar, singing a song, and said:

– Otter-night, everybody!

– Otter-what??? – Asked Satín.

– "Good evening," dear, he's saying good evening to you. He thinks that we are all otters, and he talks to us in that language. – Said the older heron.

– Oh…! "otter-night." Otter, what's your name? – Asked the traveler.

– My name is Love. – Said the otter in a singsong voice.

– Love? – Satín asked him, surprised.

– Yes, Love. I love all the beautiful things in life and I will sing about them to you and play my guitar… "I otter-love the otter of my life…I otter-love the otter of my love...and I, Love, sing to you from my heart."

– Oh, how romantic! – Said the two herons at the same time.

– You otter-love? – Satín, the traveler, asked again.

– Yes, you'll understand when you grow up. For now, enjoy every beautiful thing you encounter on your long journey. – Said the otter.

– I will! I will "otter-love" everyone in my path. Yaaayyyyy!

Satín danced, sang, and even played the guitar. The very mutty mutt was very pleased with this new world he had found. It was time to leave and continue on his journey. Satín cheerfully said goodbye to his new friends and left with his backpack on his back and his sunglasses on.

The days turned into months, and the months turned into years, as the summers, falls, and winters came and went. The pages of his notebook were all full, and the camera, which he had bought in one of the kingdoms he visited, never stopped flashing. Having gathered enough facts to show Brutos the truth of Beauty the Turtle's stories, he decided to return home to his own kingdom.

Five years had passed since the inhabitants of the kingdom had bid farewell to our hero with their song:

Satín, the traveling mutt!
Satín, the eternal traveler.
Satín, come back to your kingdom…and tell us the story!
Tra-la-la-laa Tra-la-la-laaaaa…

And Satín, still tra-la-la-ing, ran with excitement to see them. On the road he saw the sign with the name of his kingdom, and he recognized the inhabitants who came his way on the path. And he began to shout: I am Satín, the world-traveler!!!

Everyone began to whisper. Many thought that he was dead. But no, it was Satín, the very mutty mutt, who had returned full of stories.

Brutos, who was in the middle of his exercise routine in the woods and mountains, as always, paused at the stream:

Tell me, honest stream, who is the most beautiful of them all?

Brutos, Brutos... you know that you are beautiful; but Satín, the very mutty mutt, is even more beautiful than you!
– The honest stream replied.

When he heard this, Brutos became enraged. He lunged at the stream with all the fury he had inside himself. – Splash, splash, splash – went the water against his body, as he whirled furiously and chomped wildly at the water.

The honest stream let him calm down and waited until he was exhausted enough to listen: – **Brutos, you are a handsome, strong, brave dog with abilities that many would envy, but nevertheless, you have become stuck in time and you have never explored beyond the borders of your knowledge. We come to this world to learn, and that is what will make us eternal. Share everything you know and you will learn as well. Physical beauty will fade someday, but knowledge will not. And the more knowledge you have, the more beautiful you will become.**

Brutos, stunned by the words of the honest stream, decided to go and walk through the forest. His rage had gone and all that remained were the words he had just heard, which echoed in his head. He kept walking, and in the distance he heard a great commotion in the kingdom. He slowly got closer and saw in the distance the admiration that everyone felt for the traveler. He had never felt admired in that way.

Satín ran to hug Beauty the Turtle and stuttered with excitement as he told her of his experiences on the road. He took out his map and showed everyone the marvels he had found during his trip around the world.

Satín looked around and shouted: – **Brutos! Where is Brutos?**

And there, with drooping ears and a tucked tail, came Brutos, mighty and statuesque. Having reflected on what he had heard from the honest stream, and without saying a word, Brutos took Satín in his arms, lifted him high into the air, and shouted: – **Long live Satín! Long live the traveling mutt!** And everyone joined in and cheered along with Brutos! – **Hooray!**

– The laughter and singing continued into the night to celebrate the traveler's return.

From that day forward, Brutos and Satín, the very mutty mutt, were great friends who shared everything they knew with each other. Satín learned how to become a strong dog with Brutos, and Brutos opened his ears to hear all the stories from his friend who had conquered the world. And together they decided to establish a school in the kingdom to share everything they knew with others.

Brutos is the trainer and head of physical education. Satín is the explorer and travel guide. And Beauty the Turtle is the secretary who coordinates all the training exercises and explorations.

All of this made Satín's parents very proud of their son, the very mutty mutt. Brutos learned that the world was much larger than his kingdom and that beauty comes from within ...even though he still didn't totally understand that part.

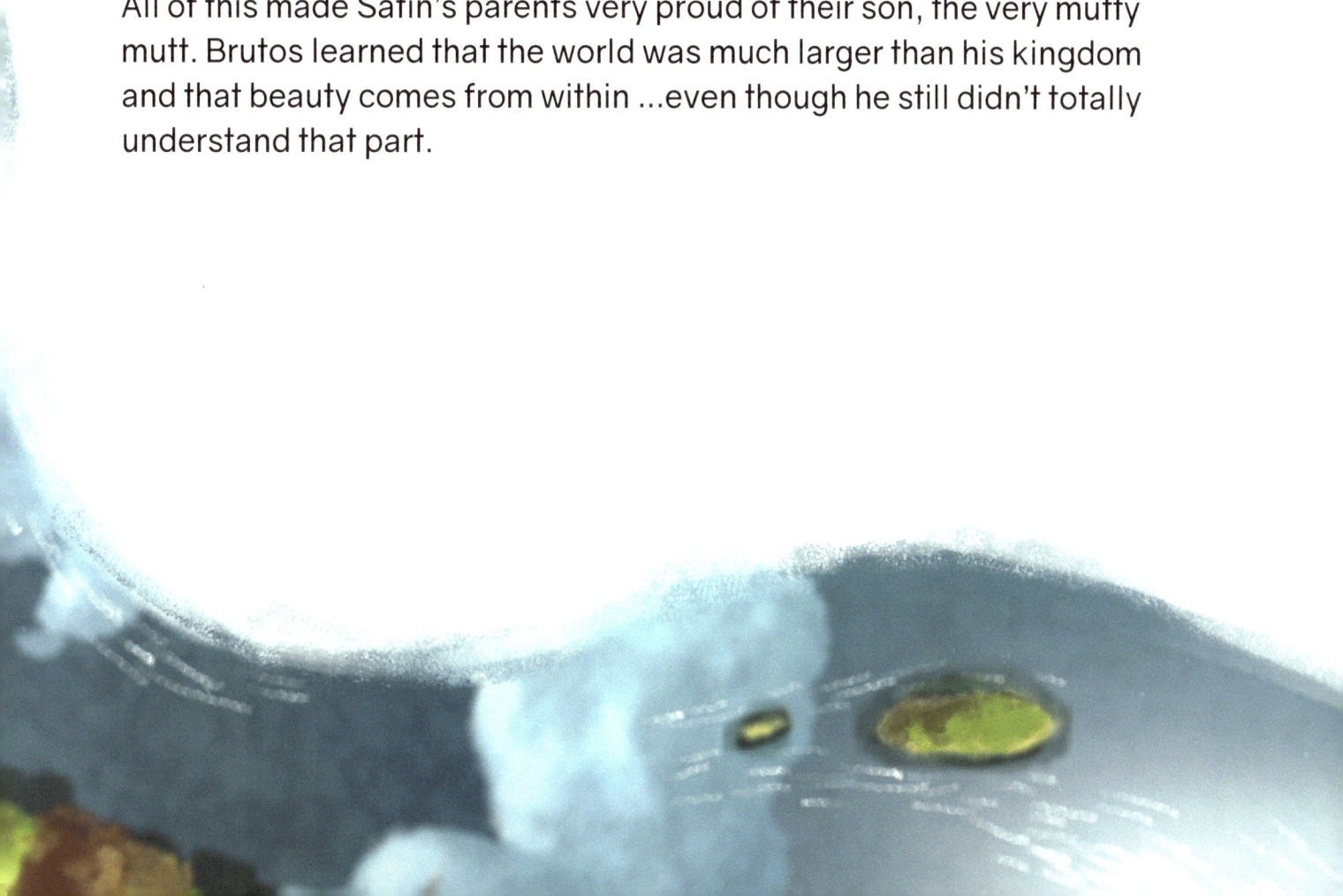

Brutos left the gym and ran across a pretty little dog wagging her tail.

– Hey there, beautiful!

Brutos, Brutos! – Shouted the stream in the distance.

– Yes, I know, I know! ...true beauty is on the inside!

And that's the end of the story! And the next story, my friend, is just beginning...!

Where did this dream begin?

One weekend in August of 2016, a little mutt appeared in my head and started jumping around. He jumped around so much that he landed right on the pages on the table. Full of joy, I invited him to write about his travels throughout the kingdoms.

My husband was the first to support us. He became our aesthetic assessor, looking after the image of every character in the story. He is my eternal traveling companion!

My mother, a firsthand witness to my youthful mischief, was my inspiration for doing this project. She, along with my father, shared in the joy of what we had made.

Rolando Martínez and Daniel Reyes helped us with the design. They illustrated and gave life, with exquisite creativity, to my Satín in his journeys through the kingdom.

Thanks to Adria Alfonso and Iliana Artidiello, who lent us their time and intellect. Their dedication was very important to this story.

So many people have given me encouragement that there's not enough room to thank them all. I want to mention Rosemary Cortes, my #1 fan and long-time friend, and all my friends on Facebook who sent me messages of love, care, and congratulations the first time we revealed the image of Satín the traveler to the public. Thanks to each and every one of you who made us love our project even more.

Welcome to the world of Satín!

"…Dedicated to Papoche, my stray dog for many years…"

To Papoche

My dog, who arrived one Sunday morning on my corner, afraid, sick, and hurt...traumatized by all the abuses he had suffered. My stray dog, who took three days to let me stroke him, who took three more to cross the threshold of the door I left open for him. The dog I healed and loved. My dog who became beautiful, and who blessed us with such happiness and loyalty. Who was the unconditional friend of my father, who cared for him and was with him every day of his happy new life. My dog who, wherever he is, will always be my dog.

I dedicate this story to you!

satin

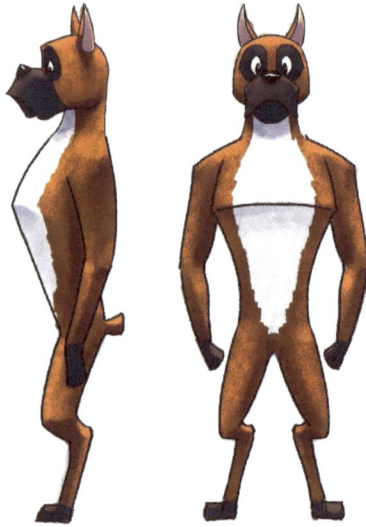

Brutos

Beauty

Advedture's characteres

Blue   Herons   Love

www.ingramcontent.com/pod-product-compliance
Lightning Source LLC
Chambersburg PA
CBHW042059040426
42448CB00002B/69